The Secrets of Enoch

By Enoch

Copyright © 2020 Lamp of Trismegistus. All rights reserved. No part of this publication may be reproduced or transmitted in any form or by any means, electronic or mechanical, including photocopying, recording, or by any information storage and retrieval system, without permission in writing from Lamp of Trismegistus. Reviewers may quote brief passages.

ISBN: 978-1-63118-449-9

Christian Apocrypha Series

Other Books in this Series and Related Titles

The Gospel of the Nativity of Mary by St. Matthew (978-1-63118-448-2)

The Testament of Abraham by Abraham (978-1-63118-441-3)

Book of Dreams by Enoch (978-1-63118-437-6)

The Book of Astronomical Secrets by Enoch (978-1-63118-443-7)

Psalms of Solomon by King Solomon (978-1-63118-439-0)

The Lives of Adam and Eve by Moses (978-1-63118-414-7)

The First and Second Gospels of the Infancy of Jesus Christ by Thomas and James (978-1-63118-415-4)

Lost Chapters of the Book of Daniel and Related Writings by Daniel (978-1-63118-417-8)

The Testament of Moses by Moses (978-1-63118-440-6)

The Book of the Watchers by Enoch (978-1-63118-416-1)

The Book of Parables by Enoch (978-1-63118-429-1)

Masonic Symbolism of Easter and the Christ in Masonry by various authors (978-1-63118-434-5)

A Few Masonic Sermons by A. C. Ward & Bascom B. Clarke (978-1-63118-435-2)

Masonic Symbolism of King Solomon's Temple by Albert G. Mackey & others (978-1-63118-442-0)

Audio Versions are also Available on Audible and iTunes

Table of Contents

Introduction...7
Prologue...9
Chapter I...11
Chapter II...13
Chapter III...14
Chapter IV...15
Chapter V...16
Chapter VI...17
Chapter VII...18
Chapter VIII...19
Chapter IX...21
Chapter X...22
Chapter XI...23
Chapter XII...24
Chapter XIII...25
Chapter XIV...26
Chapter XV...27
Chapter XVI...28
Chapter XVII...30
Chapter XVIII...31
Chapter XIX...33
Chapter XX...34
Chapter XXI...35
Chapter XXII...37
Chapter XXIII...39
Chapter XXIV...40
Chapter XXV...41
Chapter XXVI...42
Chapter XXVII...43
Chapter XXVIII...44
Chapter XXIX...45
Chapter XXX...46
Chapter XXXI...49
Chapter XXXII...50
Chapter XXXIII...51

Chapter XXXIV...53
Chapter XXXV...54
Chapter XXXVI...55
Chapter XXXVII...56
Chapter XXXVIII...57
Chapter XXXIX...58
Chapter XL...60
Chapter XLI...62
Chapter XLII...63
Chapter XLIII...64
Chapter XLIV...65
Chapter XLV...66
Chapter XLVI...67
Chapter XLVII...68
Chapter XLVIII...69
Chapter XLIX...71
Chapter L...72
Chapter LI...73
Chapter LII...74
Chapter LIII...76
Chapter LIV...77
Chapter LV...78
Chapter LVI...79
Chapter LVII...80
Chapter LVIII...81
Chapter LIX...82
Chapter LX...83
Chapter LXI...84
Chapter LXII...85
Chapter LXIII...86
Chapter LXIV...87
Chapter LXV...88
Chapter LXVI...90
Chapter LXVII...92
Chapter LXVIII...93

Introduction

The Apocrypha are a loosely knit series of books, written by early vanguards of Christianity (covering the eras of both the old and new testaments), and which comprise somewhere between about a dozen to several hundred titles, depending on whom you ask and how that person defines "Apocrypha." A small selection of these can still be found included in the Catholic bible, while a majority of the books in question, were abandoned by church officials in the early centuries of Christianity. Many of these apocryphal books were originally considered canon by early followers of Christ, in the first four centuries following his birth. It wasn't until the meeting of the Council of Nicaea in 325, that Emperor Constantine and a group of roughly 300 church bishops, gathered together with the goal of defining, standardizing and unifying an otherwise splintering Christianity, that many of these writings ceased to be included in the newly established canon. Enjoy then, this book as an example, of just one of the many books of the Christian Apocrypha, and be sure to check out other titles in this series.

Prologue

Who is Enoch and why is he so important?

Jude 1:14 describes Enoch as being the seventh generation of man from Adam, while also making reference to Enoch's ability to prophesize. Enoch was born on Seth's side of Adam and Eve's lineage and was the great grandfather of Noah. References to him in the Bible are sparse, but he is most well-known for not having died but instead for having walked away with God. In some Christian and Jewish traditions Enoch is also considered to be a scribe and to have been ordained as a priest by Adam.

Perhaps because of Enoch's unique departure from Earth into heaven, there was a rich tradition of exploring what Enoch's life was like, upon leaving Earth. The events of his time in heaven were often explored in classic rabbinical literature as well as the three primary apocryphal books with his name attached to them, of which this is the second. Some modern churches continue to embrace Enoch's importance, including the Ethiopian Orthodox Church and perhaps more notably, the Latter Day Saints.

The content of this piece covers Enoch's journey through the multiple heavens, meeting the angels Gabriel and Michael, Enoch instructing Methuselah and his other sons on moral and ethical lessons, which he had written out in 366 books and which he eventually passes on to Methuselah and his other sons, so that his teachings wouldn't be lost and finally, Enoch's eventual assumption into heaven.

The Secrets of Enoch likely dates to the first century A.D. and was part of the Old Slavonic Bible, and like nearly all texts of the biblical Apocrypha, the original author of this text has been lost to time; however, R. H. Charles prepared this translation in 1896.

Chapter I

There was a wise man, a great artificer, and the Lord conceived love for him and received him, that he should behold the uppermost dwellings and be an eye-witness of the wise and great and inconceivable and immutable realm of God Almighty, of the very wonderful and glorious and bright and many-eyed station of the Lord's servants, and of the inaccessible throne of the Lord, and of the degrees and manifestations of the incorporeal hosts, and of the ineffable ministration of the multitude of the elements, and of the various apparition and inexpressible singing of the host of Cherubim, and of the boundless light.

At that time, he said, when my one hundred and sixty-fifth year was completed, I begat my son Methuselah.

After this too I lived two hundred years and completed of all the years of my life three hundred and sixty-five years.

On the first day of the month I was in my house alone and was resting on my bed and slept.

And when I was asleep, great distress came up into my heart, and I was weeping with my eyes in sleep, and I could not understand what this distress was, or what would happen to me.

And there appeared to me two men, exceeding big, so that I never saw such on earth; their faces were shining like the sun, their eyes too were like a burning light, and from their lips was fire coming forth with clothing and singing of various kinds in appearance purple, their wings were brighter than gold, their hands whiter than snow.

They were standing at the head of my bed and began to call me by my name.

And I arose from my sleep and saw clearly those two men standing in front of me.

And I saluted them and was seized with fear and the appearance of my face was changed from terror, and those men said to me:

Have courage, Enoch, do not fear; the eternal God sent us to you, and lo! You shalt today ascend with us into heaven, and you shall tell your sons and all your household all that they shall do without you on earth in your house, and let no one seek you till the Lord return you to them.

And I made haste to obey them and went out from my house, and made to the doors, as it was ordered me, and summoned my sons Methuselah and Regim and Gaidad and made known to them all the marvels those men had told me.

Chapter II

Listen to me, my children, I know not whither I go, or what will befall me; now therefore, my children, I tell you: turn not from God before the face of the vain, who made not Heaven and earth, for these shall perish and those who worship them, and may the Lord make confident your hearts in the fear of him. And now, my children, let no one think to seek me, until the Lord return me to you.

Chapter III

It came to pass, when Enoch had told his sons, that the angels took him on to their wings and bore him up on to the first heaven and placed him on the clouds. And there I looked, and again I looked higher, and saw the ether, and they placed me on the first heaven and showed me a very great Sea, greater than the earthly sea.

Chapter IV

They brought before my face the elders and rulers of the stellar orders, and showed me two hundred angels, who rule the stars and their services to the heavens, and fly with their wings and come round all those who sail.

Chapter V

And here I looked down and saw the treasure-houses of the snow, and the angels who keep their terrible store-houses, and the clouds whence they come out and into which they go.

Chapter VI

They showed me the treasure-house of the dew, like oil of the olive, and the appearance of its form, as of all the flowers of the earth; further many angels guarding the treasure-houses of these things, and how they are made to shut and open.

Chapter VII

And those men took me and led me up on to the second heaven, and showed me darkness, greater than earthly darkness, and there I saw prisoners hanging, watched, awaiting the great and boundless judgment, and these angel spirits were dark-looking, more than earthly darkness, and incessantly making weeping through all hours.

And I said to the men who were with me: Wherefore are these incessantly tortured? They answered me: These are God's apostates, who obeyed not God's commands, but took counsel with their own will, and turned away with their prince, who also is fastened on the fifth heaven.

And I felt great pity for them, and they saluted me, and said to me: Man of God, pray for us to the Lord; and I answered to them: Who am I, a mortal man, that I should pray for angel spirits? Who knows whither I go, or what will befall me? Or who will pray for me?

Chapter VIII

And those men took me thence, and led me up on to the third heaven, and placed me there; and I looked downwards, and saw the produce of these places, such as has never been known for goodness.

And I saw all the sweet-flowering trees and beheld their fruits, which were sweet-smelling, and all the foods borne by them bubbling with fragrant exhalation.

And in the midst of the trees that of life, in that place whereon the Lord rests, when he goes up into paradise; and this tree is of ineffable goodness and fragrance, and adorned more than every existing thing; and on all sides it is in form gold-looking and vermilion and fire-like and covers all, and it has produce from all fruits.

Its root is in the garden at the earth's end.

And paradise is between corruptibility and incorruptibility.

And two springs come out which send forth honey and milk, and their springs send forth oil and wine, and they separate into four parts, and go round with quiet course, and go down into the PARADISE OF EDEN, between corruptibility and incorruptibility.

And thence they go forth along the earth, and have a revolution to their circle even as other elements.

And here there is no unfruitful tree, and every place is blessed.

And there are three hundred angels very bright, who keep the garden, and with incessant sweet singing and never-silent voices serve the Lord throughout all days and hours.

And I said: How very sweet is this place, and those men said to me:

Chapter IX

This place, O Enoch, is prepared for the righteous, who endure all manner of offence from those that exasperate their souls, who avert their eyes from iniquity, and make righteous judgment, and give bread to the hungering, and cover the naked with clothing, and raise up the fallen, and help injured orphans, and who walk without fault before the face of the Lord, and serve him alone, and for them is prepared this place for eternal inheritance.

Chapter X

And those two men led me up on to the Northern side, and showed me there a very terrible place, and there were all manner of tortures in that place: cruel darkness and un-illumined gloom, and there is no light there, but murky fire constantly flaming aloft, and there is a fiery river coming forth, and that whole place is everywhere fire, and everywhere there is frost and ice, thirst and shivering, while the bonds are very cruel, and the angels spirits fearful and merciless, bearing angry weapons, merciless torture, and I said:

Woe, woe, how very terrible is this place.

And those men said to me: This place, O Enoch, is prepared for those who dishonor God, who on earth practice sin against nature, which is child-corruption after the sodomitic fashion, magic-making, enchantments and devilish witchcrafts, and who boast of their wicked deeds, stealing, lies, calumnies, envy, rancor, fornication, murder, and who, accursed, steal the souls of men, who, seeing the poor take away their goods and themselves wax rich, injuring them for other men's goods; who being able to satisfy the empty, made the hungering to die; being able to clothe, stripped the naked; and who knew not their creator, and bowed to the soulless and lifeless gods, who cannot see nor hear, vain gods, who also built hewn images and bow down to unclean handiwork, for all these is prepared this place among these, for eternal inheritance.

Chapter XI

Those men took me, and led me up on to the fourth heaven, and showed me all the successive goings, and all the rays of the light of sun and moon.

And I measure their goings, and compared their light, and saw that the sun's light is greater than the moon's.

Its circle and the wheels on which it goes always, like the wind going past with very marvelous speed, and day and night it has no rest.

Its passage and return are accompanied by four great stars, and each star has under it a thousand stars, to the right of the sun's wheel, and by four to the left, each having under it a thousand stars, altogether eight thousand, issuing with the sun continually.

And by day fifteen myriads of angels attend it, and by night a thousand.

And six-winged ones issue with the angels before the sun's wheel into the fiery flames, and a hundred angels kindle the sun and set it alight.

Chapter XII

And I looked and saw other flying elements of the sun, whose names are Phoenixes and Chalkydri, marvelous and wonderful, with feet and tails in the form of a lion, and a crocodile's head, their appearance is empurpled, like the rainbow; their size is nine hundred measures, their wings are like those of angels, each has twelve, and they attend and accompany the sun, bearing heat and dew, as it is ordered them from God.

Thus the sun revolves and goes, and rises under the heaven, and its course goes under the earth with the light of its rays incessantly.

Chapter XIII

Those men bore me away to the east, and placed me at the sun's gates, where the sun goes forth according to the regulation of the seasons and the circuit of the months of the whole year, and the number of the hours day and night.

And I saw six gates open, each gate having sixty-one stadia and a quarter of one stadium, and I measured them truly, and understood their size to be so much, through which the sun goes forth, and goes to the west, and is made even, and rises throughout all the months, and turns back again from the six gates according to the succession of the seasons; thus the period of the whole year is finished after the returns of the four seasons.

Chapter XIV

And again those men led me away to the western parts, and showed me six great gates open corresponding to the eastern gates, opposite to where the sun sets, according to the number of the days three hundred and sixty-five and a quarter.

Thus again it goes down to the western gates, and draws away its light, the greatness of its brightness, under the earth; for since the crown of its shining is in heaven with the Lord, and guarded by four hundred angels, while the sun goes round on wheel under the earth, and stands seven great hours in night, and spends half its course under the earth, when it comes to the eastern approach in the eighth hour of the night, it brings its lights, and the crown of shining, and the sun flames forth more than fire.

Chapter XV

Then the elements of the sun, called Phoenixes and Chalkydri break into song, therefore every bird flutters with its wings, rejoicing at the giver of light, and they broke into song at the command of the Lord.

The giver of light comes to give brightness to the whole world, and the morning guard takes shape, which is the rays of the sun, and the sun of the earth goes out, and receives its brightness to light up the whole face of the earth, and they showed me this calculation of the sun's going.

And the gates which it enters, these are the great gates of the calculation of the hours of the year; for this reason the sun is a great creation, whose circuit lasts twenty-eight years, and begins again from the beginning.

Chapter XVI

Those men showed me the other course, that of the moon, twelve great gates, crowned from west to east, by which the moon goes in and out of the customary times.

It goes in at the first gate to the western places of the sun, by the first gates with thirty-one days exactly, by the second gates with thirty-one days exactly, by the third with thirty days exactly, by the fourth with thirty days exactly, by the fifth with thirty-one days exactly, by the sixth with thirty-one days exactly, by the seventh with thirty days exactly, by the eighth with thirty-one days perfectly, by the ninth with thirty-one days exactly, by the tenth with thirty days perfectly, by the eleventh with thirty-one days exactly, by the twelfth with twenty-eight days exactly.

And it goes through the western gates in the order and number of the eastern, and accomplishes the three hundred and sixty-five and a quarter days of the solar year, while the lunar year has three hundred fifty-four, and there are wanting to it twelve days of the solar circle, which are the lunar epacts of the whole year.

Thus, too, the great circle contains five hundred and thirty-two years.

The quarter of a day is omitted for three years, the fourth fulfills it exactly.

Therefore they are taken outside of heaven for three years and are not added to the number of days, because they change the time of the years to two new months towards completion, to two others towards diminution.

And when the western gates are finished, it returns and goes to the eastern to the lights, and goes thus day and night about the heavenly circles, lower than all circles, swifter than the heavenly winds, and spirits and elements and angels flying; each angel has six wings.

It has a sevenfold course in nineteen years.

Chapter XVII

In the midst of the heavens I saw armed soldiers, serving the Lord, with tympana and organs, with incessant voice, with sweet voice, with sweet and incessant voice and various singing, which it is impossible to describe, and which astonishes every mind, so wonderful and marvelous is the singing of those angels, and I was delighted listening to it.

Chapter XVIII

The men took me on to the fifth heaven and placed me, and there I saw many and countless soldiers, called Grigori, of human appearance, and their size was greater than that of great giants and their faces withered, and the silence of their mouths perpetual, and their was no service on the fifth heaven, and I said to the men who were with me:

Wherefore are these very withered and their faces melancholy, and their mouths silent, and wherefore is there no service on this heaven?

And they said to me: These are the Grigori, who with their prince Satan rejected the Lord of light, and after them are those who are held in great darkness on the second heaven, and three of them went down on to earth from the Lord's throne, to the place Ermon, and broke through their vows on the shoulder of the hill Ermon and saw the daughters of men how good they are, and took to themselves wives, and befouled the earth with their deeds, who in all times of their age made lawlessness and mixing, and giants are born and marvelous big men and great enmity.

And therefore God judged them with great judgment, and they weep for their brethren and they will be punished on the Lord's great day.

And I said to the Grigori: I saw your brethren and their works, and their great torments, and I prayed for them, but the Lord has condemned them to be under earth till the existing heaven and earth shall end forever.

And I said: Wherefore do you wait, brethren, and do not serve before the Lord's face, and have not put your services before the Lord's face, lest you anger your Lord utterly?

And they listened to my admonition, and spoke to the four ranks in heaven, and lo! As I stood with those two men four trumpets trumpeted together with great voice, and the Grigori broke into song with one voice, and their voice went up before the Lord pitifully and affectingly.

Chapter XIX

And thence those men took me and bore me up on to the sixth heaven, and there I saw seven bands of angels, very bright and very glorious, and their faces shining more than the sun's shining, glistening, and there is no difference in their faces, or behavior, or manner of dress; and these make the orders, and learn the goings of the stars, and the alteration of the moon, or revolution of the sun, and the good government of the world.

And when they see evildoing they make commandments and instruction, and sweet and loud singing, and all songs of praise.

These are the archangels who are above angels, measure all life in heaven and on earth, and the angels who are appointed over seasons and years, the angels who are over rivers and sea, and who are over the fruits of the earth, and the angels who are over every grass, giving food to all, to every living thing, and the angels who write all the souls of men, and all their deeds, and their lives before the Lord's face; in their midst are six Phoenixes and six Cherubim and six six-winged ones continually with one voice singing one voice, and it is not possible to describe their singing, and they rejoice before the Lord at his footstool.

Chapter XX

And those two men lifted me up thence on to the seventh heaven, and I saw there a very great light, and fiery troops of great archangels, incorporeal forces, and dominions, orders and governments, Cherubim and seraphim, thrones and many-eyed ones, nine regiments, the ioanit stations of light, and I became afraid, and began to tremble with great terror, and those men took me, and led me after them, and said to me:

Have courage, Enoch, do not fear, and showed me the Lord from afar, sitting on His very high throne. For what is there on the tenth heaven, since the Lord dwells there?

On the tenth heaven is God, in the Hebrew tongue he is called Aravat.

And all the heavenly troops would come and stand on the ten steps according to their rank, and would bow down to the Lord, and would again go to their places in joy and felicity, singing songs in the boundless light with small and tender voices, gloriously serving him.

Chapter XXI

And the Cherubim and seraphim standing about the throne, the six-winged and many-eyed ones do not depart, standing before the Lord's face doing his will, and cover his whole throne, singing with gentle voice before the Lord's face: Holy, holy, holy, Lord Ruler of Sabaoth, heavens and earth are full of Your glory.

When I saw all these things, those men said to me: Enoch, thus far is it commanded us to journey with you, and those men went away from me and thereupon I saw them not.

And I remained alone at the end of the seventh heaven and became afraid, and fell on my face and said to myself: Woe is me, what has befallen me?

And the Lord sent one of his glorious ones, the archangel Gabriel, and he said to me: Have courage, Enoch, do not fear, arise before the Lord's face into eternity, arise, come with me.

And I answered him, and said in myself: My Lord, my soul is departed from me, from terror and trembling, and I called to the men who led me up to this place, on them I relied, and it is with them I go before the Lord's face.

And Gabriel caught me up, as a leaf caught up by the wind, and placed me before the Lord's face.

And I saw the eighth heaven, which is called in the Hebrew tongue Muzaloth, changer of the seasons, of drought, and of wet, and of the twelve constellations of the circle of the firmament, which are above the seventh heaven.

And I saw the ninth heaven, which is called in Hebrew Kuchavim, where are the heavenly homes of the twelve constellations of the circle of the firmament.

Chapter XXII

On the tenth heaven, which is called Aravoth, I saw the appearance of the Lord's face, like iron made to glow in fire, and brought out, emitting sparks, and it burns.

Thus in a moment of eternity I saw the Lord's face, but the Lord's face is ineffable, marvelous and very awful, and very, very terrible.

And who am I to tell of the Lord's unspeakable being, and of his very wonderful face? And I cannot tell the quantity of his many instructions, and various voices, the Lord's throne is very great and not made with hands, nor the quantity of those standing round him, troops of Cherubim and seraphim, nor their incessant singing, nor his immutable beauty, and who shall tell of the ineffable greatness of his glory.

And I fell prone and bowed down to the Lord, and the Lord with his lips said to me:

Have courage, Enoch, do not fear, arise and stand before my face into eternity.

And the archistratege Michael lifted me up, and led me to before the Lord's face.

And the Lord said to his servants tempting them: Let Enoch stand before my face into eternity, and the glorious ones bowed down to the Lord, and said: Let Enoch go according to Your word.

And the Lord said to Michael: Go and take Enoch from

out of his earthly garments, and anoint him with my sweet ointment, and put him into the garments of My glory.

And Michael did thus, as the Lord told him. He anointed me, and dressed me, and the appearance of that ointment is more than the great light, and his ointment is like sweet dew, and its smell mild, shining like the sun's ray, and I looked at myself, and I was like one of his glorious ones.

And the Lord summoned one of his archangels by name Pravuil, whose knowledge was quicker in wisdom than the other archangels, who wrote all the deeds of the Lord; and the Lord said to Pravuil: Bring out the books from my storehouses, and a reed of quick-writing, and give it to Enoch, and deliver to him the choice and comforting books out of your hand.

Chapter XXIII

And he was telling me all the works of heaven, earth and sea, and all the elements, their passages and goings, and the thunderings of the thunders, the sun and moon, the goings and changes of the stars, the seasons, years, days, and hours, the risings of the wind, the numbers of the angels, and the formation of their songs, and all human things, the tongue of every human song and life, the commandments, instructions, and sweet-voiced singings, and all things that it is fitting to learn.

And Pravuil told me: All the things that I have told you, we have written. Sit and write all the souls of mankind, however many of them are born, and the places prepared for them to eternity; for all souls are prepared to eternity, before the formation of the world.

And all double thirty days and thirty nights, and I wrote out all things exactly, and wrote three hundred and sixty-six books.

Chapter XXIV

And the Lord summoned me, and said to me: Enoch, sit down on my left with Gabriel.

And I bowed down to the Lord, and the Lord spoke to me: Enoch, beloved, all that you see, all things that are standing finished I tell to you even before the very beginning, all that I created from non-being, and visible things from invisible things.

Hear, Enoch, and take in these my words, for not to My angels have I told my secret, and I have not told them their rise, nor my endless realm, nor have they understood my creating, which I tell you today.

For before all things were visible, I alone used to go about in the invisible things, like the sun from east to west, and from west to east.

But even the sun has peace in itself, while I found no peace, because I was creating all things, and I conceived the thought of placing foundations, and of creating visible creation.

Chapter XXV

I commanded in the very lowest parts, that visible things should come down from invisible, and Adoil came down very great, and I beheld him, and lo! He had a belly of great light.

And I said to him: Become undone, Adoil, and let the visible come out of you.

And he came undone, and a great light came out. And I was in the midst of the great light, and as there is born light from light, there came forth a great age, and showed all creation, which I had thought to create.

And I saw that it was good.

And I placed for myself a throne, and took my seat on it, and said to the light: Go thence up higher and fix yourself high above the throne, and be a foundation to the highest things.

And above the light there is nothing else, and then I bent up and looked up from my throne.

Chapter XXVI

And I summoned the very lowest a second time, and said: Let Archas come forth hard, and he came forth hard from the invisible.

And Archas came forth, hard, heavy, and very red.

And I said: Be opened, Archas, and let there be born from you, and he came undone, an age came forth, very great and very dark, bearing the creation of all lower things, and I saw that it was good and said to him:

Go thence down below, and make yourself firm, and be a foundation for the lower things, and it happened and he went down and fixed himself, and became the foundation for the lower things, and below the darkness there is nothing else.

Chapter XXVII

And I commanded that there should be taken from light and darkness, and I said: Be thick, and it became thus, and I spread it out with the light, and it became water, and I spread it out over the darkness, below the light, and then I made firm the waters, that is to say the bottomless, and I made foundation of light around the water, and created seven circles from inside, and imaged the water like crystal wet and dry, that is to say like glass, and as for the waters and the other elements, I showed each one of them its road, and the seven stars each one of them in its heaven, that they go thus, and I saw that it was good.

And I separated between light and between darkness, that is to say in the midst of the water hither and thither, and I said to the light, that it should be the day, and to the darkness, that it should be the night, and there was evening and there was morning the first day.

Chapter XXVIII

And then I made firm the heavenly circle, and made that the lower water which is under heaven collect itself together, into one whole, and that the chaos become dry, and it became so.

Out of the waves I created rock hard and big, and from the rock I piled up the dry, and the dry I called earth, and the midst of the earth I called abyss, that is to say the bottomless, I collected the sea in one place and bound it together with a yoke.

And I said to the sea: Behold I give you your eternal limits, and you shalt not break loose from your component parts.

Thus I made fast the firmament. This day I called the first day of creation.

Chapter XXIX

And for all the heavenly troops I imagined the image and essence of fire, and my eye looked at the very hard, firm rock, and from the gleam of my eye the lightning received its wonderful nature, which is both fire in water and water in fire, and one does not put out the other, nor does the one dry up the other, therefore the lightning is brighter than the sun, softer than water and firmer than hard rock.

And from the rock I cut off a great fire, and from the fire I created the orders of the incorporeal ten troops of angels, and their weapons are fiery and their raiment a burning flame, and I commanded that each one should stand in his order.

And one from out the order of angels, having turned away with the order that was under him, conceived an impossible thought, to place his throne higher than the clouds above the earth, that he might become equal in rank to my power.

And I threw him out from the height with his angels, and he was flying in the air continuously above the bottomless.

Chapter XXX

On the third day I commanded the earth to make grow great and fruitful trees, and hills, and seed to sow, and I planted Paradise, and enclosed it, and placed as armed guardians flaming angels, and thus I created renewal.

Then came evening, and came morning the fourth day.

On the fourth day I commanded that there should be great lights on the heavenly circles.

On the first uppermost circle I placed the stars, Kruno, and on the second Aphrodit, on the third Aris, on the fifth Zoues, on the sixth Ermis, on the seventh lesser the moon, and adorned it with the lesser stars.

And on the lower I placed the sun for the illumination of day, and the moon and stars for the illumination of night.

The sun that it should go according to each constellation, twelve, and I appointed the succession of the months and their names and lives, their thunderings, and their hour-markings, how they should succeed.

Then evening came and morning came the fifth day.

On the fifth day I commanded the sea, that it should bring forth fishes, and feathered birds of many varieties, and all animals creeping over the earth, going forth over the earth on four legs, and soaring in the air, male sex and female, and every soul breathing the spirit of life.

And there came evening, and there came morning the sixth

day.

On the sixth day I commanded my wisdom to create man from seven consistencies: one, his flesh from the earth; two, his blood from the dew; three, his eyes from the sun; four, his bones from stone; five, his intelligence from the swiftness of the angels and from cloud; six, his veins and his hair from the grass of the earth; seven, his soul from my breath and from the wind.

And I gave him seven natures: to the flesh hearing, the eyes for sight, to the soul smell, the veins for touch, the blood for taste, the bones for endurance, to the intelligence enjoyment.

I conceived a cunning saying to say, I created man from invisible and from visible nature, of both are his death and life and image, he knows speech like some created thing, small in greatness and again great in smallness, and I placed him on earth, a second angel, honorable, great and glorious, and I appointed him as ruler to rule on earth and to have my wisdom, and there was none like him of earth of all my existing creatures.

And I appointed him a name, from the four component parts, from east, from west, from south, from north, and I appointed for him four special stars, and I called his name Adam, and showed him the two ways, the light and the darkness, and I told him:

This is good, and that bad, that I should learn whether he has love towards me, or hatred, that it be clear which in his race love me.

For I have seen his nature, but he has not seen his own

nature, therefore through not seeing he will sin worse, and I said After sin what is there but death?

And I put sleep into him and he fell asleep. And I took from him a rib, and created him a wife, that death should come to him by his wife, and I took his last word and called her name mother, that is to say, Eve.

Chapter XXXI

Adam has life on earth, and I created a garden in Eden in the east, that he should observe the testament and keep the command.

I made the heavens open to him, that he should see the angels singing the song of victory, and the gloomless light.

And he was continuously in paradise, and the devil understood that I wanted to create another world, because Adam was lord on earth, to rule and control it.

The devil is the evil spirit of the lower places, as a fugitive he made Sotona from the heavens as his name was Satan, thus he became different from the angels, but his nature did not change his intelligence as far as his understanding of righteous and sinful things.

And he understood his condemnation and the sin which he had sinned before, therefore he conceived thought against Adam, in such form he entered and seduced Eve, but did not touch Adam.

And I cursed ignorance, but what I had blessed previously, those I did not curse, I cursed not man, nor the earth, nor other creatures, but man's evil fruit, and his works.

Chapter XXXII

I said to him: Earth you are, and into the earth whence I took you, you shalt go, and I will not ruin you, but send you whence I took you.

Then I can again receive you at My second presence.

And I blessed all my creatures visible and invisible. And Adam was five and half hours in paradise.

And I blessed the seventh day, which is the Sabbath, on which he rested from all his works.

Chapter XXXIII

And I appointed the eighth day also, that the eighth day should be the first-created after my work, and that the first seven revolve in the form of the seventh thousand, and that at the beginning of the eighth thousand there should be a time of not-counting, endless, with neither years nor months nor weeks nor days nor hours.

And now, Enoch, all that I have told you, all that you have understood, all that you have seen of heavenly things, all that you have seen on earth, and all that I have written in books by my great wisdom, all these things I have devised and created from the uppermost foundation to the lower and to the end, and there is no counselor nor inheritor to my creations.

I am self-eternal, not made with hands, and without change.

My thought is my counselor, my wisdom and my word are made, and my eyes observe all things how they stand here and tremble with terror.

If I turn away my face, then all things will be destroyed.

And apply your mind, Enoch, and know him who is speaking to you, and take thence the books which you yourself have written.

And I give you Samuil and Raguil, who led you up, and the books, and go down to earth, and tell your sons all that I have told you, and all that you have seen, from the lower heaven up to my throne, and all the troops.

For I created all forces, and there is none that resists me or that does not subject himself to me. For all subject themselves to my monarchy, and labor for my sole rule.

Give them the books of the handwriting, and they will read them and will know me for the creator of all things, and will understand how there is no other God but me.

And let them distribute the books of your handwriting—children to children, generation to generation, nations to nations.

And I will give you, Enoch, my intercessor, the archistratege Michael, for the handwritings of your fathers Adam, Seth, Enos, Cainan, Mahaleleel, and Jared your father.

Chapter XXXIV

They have rejected my commandments and my yoke, worthless seed has come up, not fearing God, and they would not bow down to me, but have begun to bow down to vain gods, and denied my unity, and have laden the whole earth with untruths, offences, abominable lecheries, namely one with another, and all manner of other unclean wickedness, which are disgusting to relate.

And therefore I will bring down a deluge upon the earth and will destroy all men, and the whole earth will crumble together into great darkness.

Chapter XXXV

Behold from their seed shall arise another generation, much afterwards, but of them many will be very insatiate.

He who raises that generation, shall reveal to them the books of your handwriting, of your fathers, to them, to whom he must point out the guardianship of the world, to the faithful men and workers of my pleasure, who do not acknowledge my name in vain.

And they shall tell another generation, and those others having read shall be glorified thereafter, more than the first.

Chapter XXXVI

Now, Enoch, I give you the term of thirty days to spend in your house, and tell your sons and all your household, that all may hear from my face what is told them by you, that they may read and understand, how there is no other God but me.

And that they may always keep my commandments, and begin to read and take in the books of your handwriting.

And after thirty days I shall send my angel for you, and he will take you from earth and from your sons to me.

Chapter XXXVII

And the Lord called upon one of the older angels, terrible and menacing, and placed him by me, in appearance white as snow, and his hands like ice, having the appearance of great frost, and he froze my face, because I could not endure the terror of the Lord, just as it is not possible to endure a stove's fire and the sun's heat, and the frost of the air.

And the Lord said to me: Enoch, if your face be not frozen here, no man will be able to behold your face.

Chapter XXXVIII

And the Lord said to those men who first led me up: Let Enoch go down on to earth with you, and await him till the determined day.

And they placed me by night on my bed.

And Methuselah expecting my coming, keeping watch by day and by night at my bed, was filled with awe when he heard my coming, and I told him, Let all my household come together, that I tell them everything.

Chapter XXXIX

Oh my children, my beloved ones, hear the admonition of your father, as much as is according to the Lord's will.

I have been let come to you today, and announce to you, not from my lips, but from the Lord's lips, all that is and was and all that is now, and all that will be till judgment-day.

For the Lord has let me come to you, you hear therefore the words of my lips, of a man made big for you, but I am one who has seen the Lord's face, like iron made to glow from fire it sends forth sparks and burns.

You look now upon my eyes, the eyes of a man big with meaning for you, but I have seen the Lord's eyes, shining like the sun's rays and filling the eyes of man with awe.

You see now, my children, the right hand of a man that helps you, but I have seen the Lord's right hand filling heaven as he helped me.

You see the compass of my work like your own, but I have seen the Lord's limitless and perfect compass, which has no end.

You hear the words of my lips, as I heard the words of the Lord, like great thunder incessantly with hurling of clouds.

And now, my children, hear the discourses of the father of the earth, how fearful and awful it is to come before the face of the ruler of the earth, how much more terrible and awful it is to come before the face of the ruler of heaven, the judge of quick and dead, and of the heavenly troops. Who can endure that endless pain?

Chapter XL

And now, my children, I know all things, for this is from the Lord's lips, and this my eyes have seen, from beginning to end.

I know all things, and have written all things into books, the heavens and their end, and their plenitude, and all the armies and their marchings.

I have measured and described the stars, the great countless multitude of them.

What man has seen their revolutions, and their entrances? For not even the angels see their number, while I have written all their names.

And I measured the sun's circle, and measured its rays, counted the hours, I wrote down too all things that go over the earth, I have written the things that are nourished, and all seed sown and unsown, which the earth produces and all plants, and every grass and every flower, and their sweet smells, and their names, and the dwelling-places of the clouds, and their composition, and their wings, and how they bear rain and raindrops.

And I investigated all things, and wrote the road of the thunder and of the lightning, and they showed me the keys and their guardians, their rise, the way they go; it is let out gently in measure by a chain, lest by A heavy chain and violence it hurl down the angry clouds and destroy all things on earth.

I wrote the treasure-houses of the snow, and the storehouses of the cold and the frosty airs, and I observed their season's key-holder, he fills the clouds with them, and does not exhaust the treasure-houses.

And I wrote the resting-places of the winds and observed and saw how their key-holders bear weighing-scales and measures; first, they put them in one weighing-scale, then in the other the weights and let them out according to measure cunningly over the whole earth, lest by heavy breathing they make the earth to rock.

And I measured out the whole earth, its mountains, and all hills, fields, trees, stones, rivers, all existing things I wrote down, the height from earth to the seventh heaven, and downwards to the very lowest hell, and the judgment-place, and the very great, open and weeping hell.

And I saw how the prisoners are in pain, expecting the limitless judgment.

And I wrote down all those being judged by the judge, and all their judgment and sentences and all their works.

Chapter XLI

And I saw all forefathers from all time with Adam and Eve, and I sighed and broke into tears and said of the ruin of their dishonor:

Woe is me for my infirmity and for that of my forefathers, and thought in my heart and said:

Blessed is the man who has not been born or who has been born and shall not sin before the Lord's face, that he come not into this place, nor bring the yoke of this place.

Chapter XLII

I saw the key-holders and guards of the gates of hell standing, like great serpents, and their faces like extinguishing lamps, and their eyes of fire, their sharp teeth, and I saw all the Lord's works, how they are right, while the works of man are some good, and others bad, and in their works are known those who lie evilly.

Chapter XLIII

I, my children, measured and wrote out every work and every measure and every righteous judgment.

As one year is more honorable than another, so is one man more honorable than another, some for great possessions, some for wisdom of heart, some for particular intellect, some for cunning, one for silence of lip, another for cleanliness, one for strength, another for comeliness, one for youth, another for sharp wit, one for shape of body, another for sensibility, let it be heard everywhere, but there is none better than he who fears God, he shall be more glorious in time to come.

Chapter XLIV

The Lord with his hands having created man, in the likeness of his own face, the Lord made him small and great.

Whoever reviles the ruler's face, and abhors the Lord's face, has despised the Lord's face, and he who vents anger on any man without injury, the Lord's great anger will cut him down, he who spits on the face of man reproachfully, will be cut down at the Lord's great judgment.

Blessed is the man who does not direct his heart with malice against any man, and helps the injured and condemned, and raises the broken down, and shall do charity to the needy, because on the day of the great judgment every weight, every measure and every makeweight will be as in the market, that is to say they are hung on scales and stand in the market, and every one shall learn his own measure, and according to his measure shall take his reward.

Chapter XLV

Whoever hastens to make offerings before the Lord's face, the Lord for his part will hasten that offering by granting of his work.

But whoever increases his lamp before the Lord's face and make not true judgment, the Lord will not increase his treasure in the realm of the highest.

When the Lord demands bread, or candles, or the flesh of beasts, or any other sacrifice, then that is nothing; but God demands pure hearts, and with all that only, tests the heart of man.

Chapter XLVI

Hear, my people, and take in the words of my lips.

If any one bring any gifts to an earthly ruler, and have disloyal thoughts in his heart, and the ruler know this, will he not be angry with him, and not refuse his gifts, and not give him over to judgment?

Or if one man make himself appear good to another by deceit of tongue, but have evil in his heart, then will not the other understand the treachery of his heart, and himself be condemned, since his untruth was plain to all?

And when the Lord shall send a great light, then there will be judgment for the just and the unjust, and there no one shall escape notice.

Chapter XLVII

And now, my children, lay thought on your hearts, mark well the words of your father, which are all come to you from the Lord's lips.

Take these books of your father's handwriting and read them.

For the books are many, and in them you will learn all the Lord's works, all that has been from the beginning of creation, and will be till the end of time.

And if you will observe my handwriting, you will not sin against the Lord; because there is no other except the Lord, neither in heaven, nor in earth, nor in the very lowest places, nor in the one foundation.

The Lord has placed the foundations in the unknown, and has spread forth heavens visible and invisible; he fixed the earth on the waters, and created countless creatures, and who has counted the water and the foundation of the unfixed, or the dust of the earth, or the sand of the sea, or the drops of the rain, or the morning dew, or the wind's breathings? Who has filled earth and sea, and the indissoluble winter?

I cut the stars out of fire, and decorated heaven, and put it in their midst.

Chapter XLVIII

That the sun go along the seven heavenly circles, which are the appointment of one hundred and eighty-two thrones, that it go down on a short day, and again one hundred and eighty-two, that it go down on a big day, and he has two thrones on which he rests, revolving hither and thither above the thrones of the months, from the seventeenth day of the month Tsivan it goes down to the month Thevan, from the seventeenth of Thevan it goes up.

And thus it goes close to the earth, then the earth is glad and makes grow its fruits, and when it goes away, then the earth is sad, and trees and all fruits have no florescence.

All this he measured, with good measurement of hours, and fixed a measure by his wisdom, of the visible and the invisible.

From the invisible he made all things visible, himself being invisible.

Thus I make known to you, my children, and distribute the books to your children, into all your generations, and amongst the nations who shall have the sense to fear God, let them receive them, and may they come to love them more than any food or earthly sweets, and read them and apply themselves to them.

And those who understand not the Lord, who fear not God, who accept not, but reject, who do not receive the books, a terrible judgment awaits these.

Blessed is the man who shall bear their yoke and shall drag

them along, for he shall be released on the day of the great judgment.

Chapter XLIX

I swear to you, my children, but I swear not by any oath, neither by heaven nor by earth, nor by any other creature which God created.

The Lord said: There is no oath in me, nor injustice, but truth.

If there is no truth in men, let them swear by the words, Yea, yea, or else, Nay, nay.

And I swear to you, yea, yea, that there has been no man in his mother's womb, but that already before, even to each one there is a place prepared for the repose of that soul, and a measure fixed how much it is intended that a man be tried in this world.

Yea, children, deceive not yourselves, for there has been previously prepared a place for every soul of man.

Chapter L

I have put every man's work in writing and none born on earth can remain hidden nor his works remain concealed.

I see all things.

Now therefore, my children, in patience and meekness spend the number of your days, that you inherit endless life.

Endure for the sake of the Lord every wound, every injury, every evil word and attack.

If ill-requitals befall you, return them not either to neighbor or enemy, because the Lord will return them for you and be your avenger on the day of great judgment, that there be no avenging here among men.

Whoever of you spends gold or silver for his brother's sake, he will receive ample treasure in the world to come.

Injure not widows nor orphans nor strangers, lest God's wrath come upon you.

Chapter LI

Stretch out your hands to the poor according to your strength.

Hide not your silver in the earth.

Help the faithful man in affliction, and affliction will not find you in the time of your trouble.

And every grievous and cruel yoke that come upon you bear all for the sake of the Lord, and thus you will find your reward in the day of judgment.

It is good to go morning, midday, and evening into the Lord's dwelling, for the glory of your creator.

Because every breathing thing glorifies him, and every creature visible and invisible returns him praise.

Chapter LII

Blessed is the man who opens his lips in praise of God of Sabaoth and praises the Lord with his heart.

Cursed every man who opens his lips for the bringing into contempt and calumny of his neighbor, because he brings God into contempt.

Blessed is he who opens his lips blessing and praising God.

Cursed is he before the Lord all the days of his life, who opens his lips to curse and abuse.

Blessed is he who blesses all the Lord's works.

Cursed is he who brings the Lord's creation into contempt.

Blessed is he who looks down and raises the fallen.

Cursed is he who looks to and is eager for the destruction of what is not his.

Blessed is he who keeps the foundations of his fathers made firm from the beginning.

Cursed is he who perverts the decrees of his forefathers.

Blessed is he who imparts peace and love.

Cursed is he who disturbs those that love their neighbors.

Blessed is he who speaks with humble tongue and heart to all.

Cursed is he who speaks peace with his tongue, while in his heart there is no peace but a sword.

For all these things will be laid bare in the weighing-scales and in the books, on the day of the great judgment.

Chapter LIII

And now, my children, do not say: Our father is standing before God, and is praying for our sins, for there is there no helper of any man who has sinned.

You see how I wrote all works of every man, before his creation, all that is done amongst all men for all time, and none can tell or relate my handwriting, because the Lord see all imaginings of man, how they are vain, where they lie in the treasure-houses of the heart.

And now, my children, mark well all the words of your father, that I tell you, lest you regret, saying: Why did our father not tell us?

Chapter LIV

At that time, not understanding this let these books which I have given you be for an inheritance of your peace.

Hand them to all who want them, and instruct them, that they may see the Lord's very great and marvelous works.

Chapter LV

My children, behold, the day of my term and time have approached.

For the angels who shall go with me are standing before me and urge me to my departure from you; they are standing here on earth, awaiting what has been told them.

For tomorrow I shall go up on to heaven, to the uppermost Jerusalem to my eternal inheritance.

Therefore I bid you do before the Lord's face all his good pleasure.

Chapter LVI

Methuselah having answered his father Enoch, said: What is agreeable to your eyes, father, that I may make before your face, that you may bless our dwellings, and your sons, and that your people may be made glorious through you, and then that you may depart thus, as the Lord said?

Enoch answered to his son Methuselah and said: Hear, child, from the time when the Lord anointed me with the ointment of his glory, there has been no food in me, and my soul remembers not earthly enjoyment, neither do I want anything earthly.

Chapter LVII

My child Methuselah, summon all your brethren and all your household and the elders of the people, that I may talk to them and depart, as is planned for me.

And Methuselah made haste, and summoned his brethren, Regim, Riman, Uchan, Chermion, Gaidad, and all the elders of the people before the face of his father Enoch; and he blessed them, and said to them:

Chapter LVIII

Listen to me, my children, today.

In those days when the Lord came down on to earth for Adam's sake, and visited all his creatures, which he created himself, after all these he created Adam, and the Lord called all the beasts of the earth, all the reptiles, and all the birds that soar in the air, and brought them all before the face of our father Adam.

And Adam gave the names to all things living on earth.

And the Lord appointed him ruler over all, and subjected to him all things under his hands, and made them dumb and made them dull that they be commanded of man, and be in subjection and obedience to him.

Thus also the Lord created every man lord over all his possessions.

The Lord will not judge a single soul of beast for man's sake, but adjudges the souls of men to their beasts in this world; for men have a special place.

And as every soul of man is according to number, similarly beasts will not perish, nor all souls of beasts which the Lord created, till the great judgment, and they will accuse man, if he feed them ill.

Chapter LIX

Whoever defiles the soul of beasts, defiles his own soul.

For man brings clean animals to make sacrifice for sin, that he may have cure of his soul.

And if they bring for sacrifice clean animals, and birds, man has cure, he cures his soul.

All is given you for food, bind it by the four feet, that is to make good the cure, he cures his soul.

But whoever kills beast without wounds, kills his own souls and defiles his own flesh.

And he who does any beast any injury whatsoever, in secret, it is evil practice, and he defiles his own soul.

Chapter LX

He who works the killing of a man's soul, kills his own soul, and kills his own body, and there is no cure for him for all time.

He who puts a man in any snare, shall stick in it himself, and there is no cure for him for all time.

He who puts a man in any vessel, his retribution will not be wanting at the great judgment for all time.

He who works crookedly or speaks evil against any soul, will not make justice for himself for all time.

Chapter LXI

And now, my children, keep your hearts from every injustice, which the Lord hates. Just as a man asks something for his own soul from God, so let him do to every living soul, because I know all things, how in the great time to come there is much inheritance prepared for men, good for the good, and bad for the bad, without number many.

Blessed are those who enter the good houses, for in the bad houses there is no peace nor return from them.

Hear, my children, small and great! When man puts a good thought in his heart, brings gifts from his labors before the Lord's face and his hands made them not, then the Lord will turn away his face from the labor of his hand, and that man cannot find the labor of his hands.

And if his hands made it, but his heart murmur, and his heart cease not making murmur incessantly, he has not any advantage.

Chapter LXII

Blessed is the man who in his patience brings his gifts with faith before the Lord's face, because he will find forgiveness of sins.

But if he take back his words before the time, there is no repentance for him; and if the time pass and he do not of his own will what is promised, there is no repentance after death.

Because every work which man does before the time, is all deceit before men, and sin before God.

Chapter LXIII

When man clothes the naked and fills the hungry, he will find reward from God.

But if his heart murmur, he commits a double evil; ruin of himself and of that which he gives; and for him there will be no finding of reward on account of that.

And if his own heart is filled with his food and his own flesh, clothed with his own clothing, he commits contempt, and will forfeit all his endurance of poverty, and will not find reward of his good deeds.

Every proud and magniloquent man is hateful to the Lord, and every false speech, clothed in untruth; it will be cut with the blade of the sword of death, and thrown into the fire, and shall burn for all time.

Chapter LXIV

When Enoch had spoken these words to his sons, all people far and near heard how the Lord was calling Enoch. They took counsel together:

Let us go and kiss Enoch, and two thousand men came together and came to the place Achuzan where Enoch was, and his sons.

And the elders of the people, the whole assembly, came and bowed down and began to kiss Enoch and said to him:

Our father Enoch, may you be blessed of the Lord, the eternal ruler, and now bless your sons and all the people, that we may be glorified today before your face.

For you shalt be glorified before the Lord's face for all time, since the Lord chose you, rather than all men on earth, and designated you writer of all his creation, visible and invisible, and redeemed of the sins of man, and helper of your household.

Chapter LXV

And Enoch answered all his people saying: Hear, my children, before that all creatures were created, the Lord created the visible and invisible things.

And as much time as there was and went past, understand that after all that he created man in the likeness of his own form, and put into him eyes to see, and ears to hear, and heart to reflect, and intellect wherewith to deliberate.

And the Lord saw all man's works, and created all his creatures, and divided time, from time he fixed the years, and from the years he appointed the months, and from the months he appointed the days, and of days he appointed seven.

And in those he appointed the hours, measured them out exactly, that man might reflect on time and count years, months, and hours, their alternation, beginning, and end, and that he might count his own life, from the beginning until death, and reflect on his sin and write his work bad and good; because no work is hidden before the Lord, that every man might know his works and never transgress all his commandments, and keep my handwriting from generation to generation.

When all creation visible and invisible, as the Lord created it, shall end, then every man goes to the great judgment, and then all time shall perish, and the years, and thenceforward there will be neither months nor days nor hours, they will be adhered together and will not be counted.

There will be one aeon, and all the righteous who shall escape the Lord's great judgment, shall be collected in the great aeon, for the righteous the great aeon will begin, and they will live eternally, and then too there will be amongst them neither labor, nor sickness, nor humiliation, nor anxiety, nor need, nor brutality, nor night, nor darkness, but great light.

And they shall have a great indestructible wall, and a paradise bright and incorruptible, for all corruptible things shall pass away, and there will be eternal life.

Chapter LXVI

And now, my children, keep your souls from all injustice, such as the Lord hates.

Walk before his face with terror and trembling and serve him alone.

Bow down to the true God, not to dumb idols, but bow down to his similitude, and bring all just offerings before the Lord's face. The Lord hates what is unjust.

For the Lord sees all things; when man takes thought in his heart, then he counsels the intellects, and every thought is always before the Lord, who made firm the earth and put all creatures on it.

If you look to heaven, the Lord is there; if you take thought of the sea's deep and all the under-earth, the Lord is there.

For the Lord created all things. Bow not down to things made by man, leaving the Lord of all creation, because no work can remain hidden before the Lord's face.

Walk, my children, in long-suffering, in meekness, honesty, in provocation, in grief, in faith and in truth, in reliance on promises, in illness, in abuse, in wounds, in temptation, in nakedness, in privation, loving one another, till you go out from this age of ills, that you become inheritors of endless time.

Blessed are the just who shall escape the great judgment, for they shall shine forth more than the sun sevenfold, for in this world the seventh part is taken off from all, light, darkness, food, enjoyment, sorrow, paradise, torture, fire, frost, and other things; he put all down in writing, that you might read and understand.

Chapter LXVII

When Enoch had talked to the people, the Lord sent out darkness on to the earth, and there was darkness, and it covered those men standing with Enoch, and they took Enoch up on to the highest heaven, where the Lord is; and he received him and placed him before his face, and the darkness went off from the earth, and light came again.

And the people saw and understood not how Enoch had been taken, and glorified God, and found a roll in which was traced The Invisible God; and all went to their dwelling places.

Chapter LXVIII

Enoch was born on the sixth day of the month Tsivan, and lived three hundred and sixty-five years.

He was taken up to heaven on the first day of the month Tsivan and remained in heaven sixty days.

He wrote all these signs of all creation, which the Lord created, and wrote three hundred and sixty-six books, and handed them over to his sons and remained on earth thirty days, and was again taken up to heaven on the sixth day of the month Tsivan, on the very day and hour when he was born.

As every man's nature in this life is dark, so are also his conception, birth, and departure from this life.

At what hour he was conceived, at that hour he was born, and at that hour too he died.

Methuselah and his brethren, all the sons of Enoch, made haste, and erected an altar at that place called Achuzan, whence and where Enoch had been taken up to heaven.

And they took sacrificial oxen and summoned all people and sacrificed the sacrifice before the Lord's face.

All people, the elders of the people and the whole assembly came to the feast and brought gifts to the sons of Enoch.

And they made a great feast, rejoicing and making merry three days, praising God, who had given them such a sign through Enoch, who had found favor with him, and that they should hand it on to their sons from generation to generation, from age to age.

Amen.

www.ingramcontent.com/pod-product-compliance
Lightning Source LLC
LaVergne TN
LVHW041634070426
835507LV00008B/611